Kangaroos

Edel Wignell

CELEBRATION PRESS
Pearson Learning Group

Map of the World

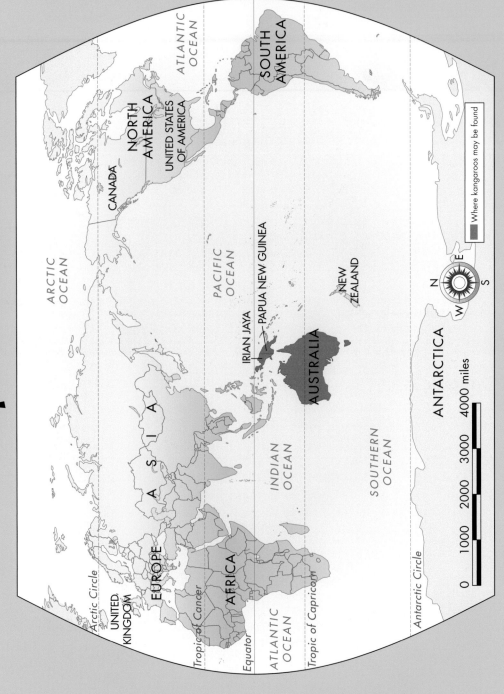

ARCTIC OCEAN

NORTH AMERICA

CANADA

UNITED STATES OF AMERICA

ATLANTIC OCEAN

SOUTH AMERICA

PACIFIC OCEAN

PAPUA NEW GUINEA

IRIAN JAYA

NEW ZEALAND

AUSTRALIA

ANTARCTICA

A S I A

EUROPE

UNITED KINGDOM

AFRICA

INDIAN OCEAN

SOUTHERN OCEAN

ATLANTIC OCEAN

Arctic Circle

Tropic of Cancer

Equator

Tropic of Capricorn

Antarctic Circle

N
W   E
S

Where kangaroos may be found

0   1000   2000   3000   4000 miles

Contents

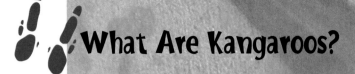

What Are Kangaroos?

Gray kangaroos are gathered near water.

Kangaroos are **mammals** found naturally only in Australia, Papua New Guinea, and Irian Jaya. There are more than fifty species grouped in two families—large kangaroos and small kangaroos.

The large kangaroo family includes red kangaroos, gray kangaroos, wallabies, pademelons, tree kangaroos, and quokkas.

Members of the small kangaroo family include bettongs, rat kangaroos, and potoroos.

A female with a **joey** in her pouch

Kangaroos Are Marsupials

Marsupials are a type of mammal that gives birth to undeveloped young. The female kangaroo, like many other marsupials, has a pouch in the front of her body to carry and nourish the undeveloped young until the joey can survive on its own.

A tree kangaroo

A potoroo

What Do Kangaroos Look Like?

Adult male red kangaroos

Most kangaroos have narrow heads, large oval ears, long noses, and dense fur. All kangaroos have strong back legs with long feet, which they use to hop.

Kangaroo tails, being large and heavy, are used for balance when hopping and for support when sitting. All kangaroos have furry tails, except for musky rat kangaroos whose tails are bare. Their **drab** coloring helps them blend into their surroundings.

Some kangaroos are taller than a human, and some are as small as a rabbit. Female kangaroos are smaller than the males.

The largest kangaroos are the male red and gray kangaroos. These large kangaroos can stand up to 6½ feet tall and weigh up to almost 200 pounds.

The smallest kangaroo is the musky rat kangaroo, which measures about 11 inches (not including its tail). This little creature weighs about 1 pound.

An adult male musky rat kangaroo

Long Leaps

Many kangaroos make huge leaps and bounds.

When you make the long jump, how far do you leap?
Large kangaroos can leap up to 30 feet. They can
sail over a fence that is 9 feet high and can race
at 37 miles per hour. The only member of the
kangaroo family that does not hop is the musky
rat kangaroo.

The kangaroo's back or hind legs have long feet, with four toes on each foot. Kangaroos hold their tails out behind them to keep their balance as they leap.

The kangaroo's hind legs have long feet.

Alarm Signals

Kangaroos are shy animals and avoid humans if they can. When danger looms, they beat on the ground with their hind feet. This alarm signal can be heard from far away by other kangaroos.

Forelegs

The paws of a gray kangaroo

Kangaroos can use their front paws like hands.

Kangaroos have short forelegs with five toes or digits on each of their small front paws. Some kangaroos use these digits as fingers to pick up food and put it into their mouths.

They also use their forelegs or front legs when they walk slowly and when they play. They engage in playful boxing with their family groups.

In a serious fight, kangaroos box with their forepaws and kick with their strong hind feet, while their tail helps them to balance.

Adult large kangaroos can protect themselves when attacked. Each hind foot has a sharp claw that can be used in defense.

Gray kangaroos boxing on a beach

Where Do Kangaroos Live?

Kangaroos are found throughout Australia, on some of the islands off the Australian north and west coasts, and in Papua New Guinea.

A rock wallaby in its natural habitat

Kangaroos Live in Various Habitats

Kind	Habitat
red kangaroos and gray kangaroos	grasslands and open woodlands
rock wallabies	stony country, among rocks
bettongs	burrows in dry scrublands
tree kangaroos	rain forests of northeastern Australia
rat kangaroos	undergrowth in rain forests
quokkas	windswept islands off the coast of Western Australia

A brush-tailed bettong

A tree kangaroo

13

What Do Kangaroos Eat?

Gray kangaroos grazing on grassland

Kangaroos have long, strong teeth. Most kangaroos are **herbivores**. They eat many different kinds of plants, but grass makes up most of their diet. They feed on plants and grasses that are full of **moisture**. Due to this diet, most kangaroos can go without drinking water for a long time.

Red kangaroos and gray kangaroos are grazers, feeding mostly on grasses. Species that live in forests—such as the swamp wallaby, tree kangaroo, and wallaroo—eat leaves, plant shoots, and twigs.

Small forest kangaroos—such as rat kangaroos, bettongs, and musky rat kangaroos—are **omnivores**. They eat insects, worms, fungi, plants, and **carrion**.

A Tasmanian bettong with its young

A Kangaroo's Day

A mob of kangaroos

Kangaroos graze in the early mornings and evenings. In the hottest part of the day, they rest or play under shady trees or bushes.

Red and gray kangaroos live in groups of ten or more males and females. These groups are called mobs.

Most of the small kangaroos are **solitary**. The mothers and their young stay together until the young are ready to live on their own.

A kangaroo mother with her young

The Boomer

The largest and strongest male of the kangaroo mob is called the boomer. It may take ten years for a male kangaroo to achieve this position, which may only last a year. Soon enough a younger, stronger male will fight the boomer and become the new leader of the mob.

Baby Kangaroos

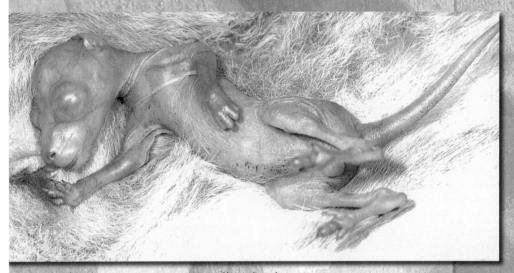

The baby kangaroo is so small at birth
that three babies can fit into a teaspoon!

Kangaroo joeys are tiny at birth, measuring less than
1 inch. The newborn is still in **embryo** form when it leaves
its mother's womb. It crawls through the mother's belly fur
to reach her pouch. It weighs less than an ounce and
is undeveloped.

In the warm pouch the joey feeds on milk. It feeds without
leaving the pouch until it is about three months old.

When the joey is about three months old, it is covered with fur and is big enough to start to leave the pouch. It eats grass and returns to the pouch to sleep. The joey may stay with its mother in her pouch until it is a year old.

Female kangaroos reach their full size at four years of age and males at ten years.

A baby kangaroo is called a joey.

Large kangaroos can live twelve to eighteen years in the wild and up to twenty-eight years in **captivity**. The smaller species have a shorter **life span**.

Twin Kangaroo Joeys

All female kangaroos, except the musky rat kangaroo, give birth to only one young each year. The musky rat kangaroo usually has twins.

Kangaroos in Danger

When European settlers went to Australia, they cleared vast areas of land. Kangaroos lost much of their grazing habitat to introduced animals, such as sheep, cattle, and rabbits.

For many years, kangaroos were hunted for their meat, fur, and skins. The furs and skins were sold to make bags, gloves, and shoes.

Small kangaroos are easily killed by introduced predators, such as foxes and **feral** cats. Some kangaroo species have become extinct.

The endangered hare wallaby

Today, about ten species of kangaroo are endangered, including several rat kangaroos, two hare wallabies, and two nailtail wallabies.

Some of the smaller kangaroos, such as bettongs and quokkas, have been saved from extinction by scientists. They breed the animals in captivity and release them into their natural habitats.

The endangered nailtail wallaby

Protecting the Kangaroo

Legislation in all the Australian States and Territories protects the kangaroo to ensure its survival. There are harsh penalties to prevent cruelty and abuse of this animal.

Controlling Kangaroo Numbers

The red kangaroo appears on Australia's Coat of Arms.

The kangaroo is an important animal to Australians. It is shown here on Australia's Commonwealth Coat of Arms. However, in some parts of Australia, thousands of kangaroos graze in huge groups on farming land. Their numbers are so large that farmers regard them as pests.

Large kangaroo populations also cause damage to the natural environment. This damage threatens the survival of other native animals.

To keep kangaroo numbers under control, kangaroos are shot and killed by professionals who have a special license to do so. The **culling** process is strictly controlled by government legislation.

The Kangaroo Industry

Commercial use of kangaroos is strictly **regulated** by law. Only certain numbers of the most **abundant** species may be harvested, and only by licensed hunters. Kangaroo meat is high in protein and iron and is low in cholestrol. Australia exports this meat to more than twenty-five countries. Some kangaroo meat is used as pet food, and skins are collected, mostly for export.

Glossary

abundant	more than enough; in large quantity
captivity	kept safe, fed, and looked after; unable to escape
carrion	dead flesh
culling	killing a number of animals from a group to stop the group from becoming too large
drab	a dull yellowish brown
embryo	the undeveloped offspring of an animal before birth
feral	an animal living in the wild which usually is tame, like a cat
herbivores	animals that feed only on plants
joey	a young kangaroo
life span	the length of time an animal or a human is likely to live
mammals	warmblooded animals that give birth to live babies that are fed milk
moisture	wetness; water in small drops on a surface
omnivore	an animal that feeds on both plants and meat
regulated	controlled by laws or rules
solitary	being alone

Index